MONKEY COLORING BOOK

CRYSTAL
COLORING BOOKS

COLOR TEST PAGE

COLOR TEST PAGE

www.ingramcontent.com/pod-product-compliance
Lightning Source LLC
Chambersburg PA
CBHW081244280526

45787CB00006B/2792